1 Ghosts

GW01463896

Paul Groves
and Nigel Grimshaw

Drawings by Martin Pitts

Edward Arnold

First published 1984 by
Edward Arnold (Publishers) Ltd
41 Bedford Square, London WC1B 3DQ

British Library Cataloguing in Publication Data
Groves, Paul
    10 ghosts.
1. Readers – Ghosts
I. Title   II. Grimshaw, Nigel
428'.6   PE1127.G/

ISBN 0-7131-0962-9

Set in 12/14 Baskerville by 𝄐 Tek Art, 55 Stanhope Road,
Croydon, Surrey CR0 5NS.
Printed in Great Britain by Spottiswoode Ballantyne Ltd, Colchester
and London

Contents

The Ghost Who Liked Babies

Looking back on this strange case the first incident was on August the 7th 1983. A woman had left her pram outside a supermarket in the High Street of Rowenstall. She came out to find it gone. Meanwhile, shoppers in the street were horrified to see a pram going down the hill on its own. A man made a grab but the pram moved sideways and he missed. It was going straight towards a busy road junction. Luckily a woman was speedier than the man and managed to grab the pram just in time. Though afterwards she said that she was sure she felt a push in the side as she grabbed it. At the time the incident was put down to a faulty brake.

The second incident occurred in a less busy part of the town. A woman watched from her window as a pram went slowly downhill towards the river. She was in a wheelchair and could not go out to it. She phoned the police on 999. They found the pram by the river's edge near some ducks. They were very puzzled as to why the pram had not gone in the river as the slope on which the pram was found was quite steep.

The third incident also occurred in a supermarket. A woman was bending over a baby going: 'Coo! Coo!' when the baby was suddenly lifted out of the pram and floated by her shoulder. She tried to grab it. The baby's mother came along at that moment and accused the woman of trying to steal her baby. They screamed at each other and the police were called by the manager. The unfortunate woman spent many hours in the police station before she was released.

The fourth incident happened when a baby disappeared from its pram in a garden and was found half a mile away in a graveyard. This was put down as a definite kidnapping until a pensioner declared that he had seen a baby 'floating' in the air near the graveyard.

The pensioner had been drinking but the local press now printed an article called 'The Ghost Who Likes Babies' based on the incidents. The national press picked this up and the story appeared in the morning papers. The small town had become famous overnight.

The mothers of the town were terrified by all this publicity. No baby was left alone outside. But then one disappeared from its cot in a bedroom. This caused tremendous panic. It was found quite unharmed in the same graveyard. Mothers started to sleep in the same rooms as their babies. Their talk in the town was of nothing else.

James 'Brains' Odunton sat at the back of the history class. He had not joined in the lesson all afternoon. The class were looking at evidence of poverty and disease in the 19th century. 'What's up, James?' asked Miss Claridge. 'You haven't contributed a thing to the lesson today. What about these photos I took?'

'Well, it has set me thinking about babies, Miss.' The girls laughed.

'What about babies?'

'Well, if we had been born in those times we would not be here now.'

The class laughed.

'You know what I mean,' said James. 'We would

have died.'

The photo in front of him was of four small headstones. Each one was in 'loving memory' of a child aged one, all from the same family.

'You're right, James. You are lucky to have been born in the nineteen seventies.'

Afterwards, in the yard, he went over to Richard and Allie. 'I've got a theory about the ghost who likes babies,' he said. 'Are you coming with me at the end of school?'

'That last theory you had about perpetual motion cost us all our pocket money for a month,' said Allie.

'No, this is an ace theory. You remember that evidence photo of the four baby graves?'

'Yes.'

'They were all in the same family.'

'So? It happened in those days.'

'I want to go and see them.'

'What for?'

'I'll tell you when we get there. Come on.'

'No!' said Richard.

'I'll buy you a Coke.'

'Okay. Coming, Allie?'

'We won't be long will we?'

'No.'

The children walked up the hill to the cemetery. As they went they passed a placard outside a news-agent's which read: 'Another baby floats in the air. Mother terrified.'

When they got there they looked in the long grass for the four graves. Allie found them. 'They're just like the photo,' she said.

'Now,' said James, 'I want you to look around here for the headstone of the mother.'

'But there are hundreds of headstones,' complained Richard. 'Why?'

'I'll tell you later. Come on we can run round.'

They looked for half an hour and could not find it.

'Good,' said James. 'We've found nothing.'

'You mean we've been wasting our time,' said Richard.

'It supports my theory,' said James. 'Now we have to go to the graveyard where the missing babies were found.'

'But that's creepy,' said Allie.

'Come on, it's a long time before it gets dark,' urged James. 'This could be great. I'll pay the bus fares.'

They took a bus to the other end of the town. When they got there Richard stayed outside and Allie went in with James. 'You don't think there are bats do you?' she said. 'It's beginning to get dark.'

'No, now look for the mother of those children. She will be something Rogers. There aren't so many headstones here.'

They poked around in the long grass. After a quarter of an hour Allie shrieked, 'I've found it! Amelia Rogers. Passed away from this life aged 65 years. 1860–1925. May she rest in peace.'

'She hasn't rested in peace has she,' said James.

'What do you mean?' asked Allie.

'I think that she's been looking for her babies,' said James. 'You see, two babies have been found here.'

'Will anyone believe us?' asked Allie.

'Let's tell Richard,' shouted James. But Richard had run off when Allie had shrieked.

'I'm going to the local paper tomorrow,' said James.

The newspaper reporter was not pleased to see this kid who had been waiting an hour. He had a deadline to meet about the football match. 'I'll give you three minutes,' he said when he finally came into the waiting room. 'Don't tell me, you want to set up a baby watching service. I've had kids on the phone all day.'

'No,' said James, 'I think I know why it happens. I have a theory backed up by evidence.'

'Well, be quick.'

As James explained his theory the newspaper reporter's glasses slid off his forehead down onto his nose. 'There's a story in this!' he exclaimed.

His article about it appeared in the next night's paper. It gripped the imagination of the town. It was debated everywhere. There was a demand that the babies should be reburied by the mother. But there was opposition from the vicar of the churchyard who did not want the graves disturbed in any way. But then two more babies disappeared and reappeared in the graveyard, so the vicar gave way to the public outcry.

The babies were reburied. The 'floatings' and the appearance of babies in the churchyard stopped. James 'Brains' Odunton became the local hero. He decided to become a professional ghost hunter when he grew up.

Looking at the story again

1 What was the first incident that happened?

2 What was the incident put down to? What suggests that it had another explanation?

3 What puzzled the police about the second incident?

4 Why was the woman in the third incident unfortunate?

5 Which incident gives the biggest clue to the mystery?

6 What caused 'tremendous panic'?

7 Why are the children not keen on James' theory at first?

8 Why is James pleased when they don't find the headstone of the mother?

9 Who is the least brave of the children?

10 Why does the reporter not want to see James?

Words

1 Use 'steal' and 'steel' in separate sentences of your own.

2 Put each of these words which are often spelt wrongly in a sentence of your own: definite; disappeared; beginning; believe.

3 What word in the passage means 'going on and on'? It begins with a 'p'.

4 What is a 'placard'?

5 'Reburied' — make a list of five words that begin with 're' joined to another word. What does 're' do to some words?

Writing

1 Ghosts are usually associated with lonely places. Write a story about a ghost near an old bridge in the country.

2 Imagine that you are a policeman or woman called to incident three. Write the report that you put in your notebook.

3 Write the scene in the graveyard as a play. You can add lines to make it creepy.

4 Write an unrhymed poem called: 'Churchyard'.

5 Write a headline for the story that might appear in the local paper after James' discovery.

Dream Dog

Tony was dreaming again. He was walking through the woods with the dog. It was big and black and powerful. With the dog at his side he was happy and protected from harm. His mother's voice woke him and shattered the dream.

'Tony!'

He lay in bed and stared at the ceiling. The warm feeling of the dream vanished. He sighed. Tony! What a silly name! It was his name that had begun his troubles that first day at school.

'What's your name?' Ray Farmer had asked him.

'Tony,' he had said.

'"Tony!"' Ben Hicks – or Hickey – had sneered. 'What a wet name! You're wet, kid. D'you know that?'

'I'm not,' he said.

'Oh, yes you are,' Ray told him. He and Hickey looked at each other. 'Tony! Toe – knee! You're wet.'

'Toe!' said Hickey, stamping on his foot.

'Knee!' said Ray. He had kicked Tony then behind his knees and Tony had fallen, saving himself with his hands.

That's how it had started. And – except for the few days when Tony had pretended to be ill and stayed away from school – they had gone on bullying him ever since.

It was getting worse, too. Today he would have to get another 20p from his mother for them. He

sighed again. The dream dog had been just a dream. There wasn't now even the real dog in the doorway to talk to any more. Remembering it made him feel better for a moment, though.

When he and his mother had moved to the new town, he had passed the old dog every day on his way to school. The front doors of the houses in Clandon Street opened directly on to the pavement. The dog, large and black and fat, had always been lying there in the open door in the sun. It had friendly eyes and all round its mouth and nose its hair was greyish-white, like an old man's. When Tony had stopped that first day, it had feebly wagged its tail. Tony had patted its head. It didn't get up but it blinked its eyes and wagged its tail some more. After that Tony had stopped every time he passed and talked to it. Sometimes, when he had chocolate, he gave it a piece. It had been a friend in a new, unfriendly world.

Last week the door had been closed. He had knocked. An old man came out.

'Where's the dog?' asked Tony.

'Gone,' said the old man. 'He was old, poor old lad. He's gone. He died.'

Tony had said nothing and left. On the rest of his way to school, he had felt like crying.

Thinking about school brought Ray and Hickey back into his mind. He hated them. He wished that he was big and strong so that he could beat them up. He wished he had a dog to frighten them with. It would be like the dream dog, big and black and fierce.

'Tony!' his mother called again.

'I'm coming!' he shouted and got up.

He had tried to tell her once or twice about Ray and Hickey. He knew she had a lot of worries but she hadn't really listened to him. She had told him that he was getting to be a big boy now and should fight his own battles. It was a new school and he would soon settle down and get used to it, she had said. He hadn't dared to tell Miss Williams, the class teacher, about Ray and Hickey. He didn't know her very well and he was afraid of what the two of them might do to him afterwards if he told her.

When he was dressed, he sighed again and went slowly downstairs.

That day at school, however, was not too bad after all. Ray and Hickey had pounced on him when he got there. When he gave them the 20p he had managed to get from his mother, though, they didn't do anything to him. They had both been kept in at playtime. During the dinner hour he had hidden and kept out of their way. After school he had been one of the first out and had run most of the way home.

He was watching television when his mother came in from work. She looked tired. She was not in a very good temper because she had forgotten to buy any milk. She told him to go and fetch some from the Shopping Centre.

'Go the quick way across the park,' she said.

'The park – ?' he asked. He didn't want to go that way.

'Yes,' she said. 'Don't start arguing. You've got to be quick. They'll be closing soon. Go now.' She gave him the money.

He kept a sharp look out on his way through the park. He knew that Ray and Hickey often went there to kick a ball about or, more likely, to cause trouble.

But he saw no sign of them. On his way back he thought of other things. He wished he really did

14

have a dog. He imagined it running on ahead of him into the darkness and coming back when he called. It would be good company.

'Hello, Tony.'

'Where are you going, kid?'

The street lighting did not reach there to the middle of the park. As he rounded some bushes, Ray and Hickey suddenly appeared out of the gloom. Ray grabbed hold of the bottle of milk Tony was carrying. Tony's stomach turned over. He began to shake. He would get it from Ray and Hickey and then there would be more trouble at home when he returned without the milk.

'Want a drink, Hickey?' Ray asked. Tony hung on to the bottle.

'Leave me alone,' he said weakly. Then, without really knowing why he said it, he added, 'I'll call my dog.'

'Dog? What dog?' Ray sneered.

'It'll be a little woolly dog, if it's yours,' Hickey mocked him.

Then they both stood as if turned to stone. From behind Tony had come a growl. It was long and low, savage and blood-curdling. 'Cor!' Ray whispered. His slack hand fell away from the milk bottle. Hickey shrank back. Tony turned to find out what they were looking at.

A dog was hunched there, looking huge in a glow of cold, blue light. It was smooth-coated and black and its ears were pulled close to its large, snake-like head. Its nose was wrinkled with rage and its lips were curled back to show the long white daggers of its teeth. These sparkled with a deadly gleam and its eyes burned with green fire.

An icy chill ran through Tony at the sight of it. But, if he was frightened, Ray and Hickey were terrified. Ray with his open hands up in front of his face was whispering, 'No, no, no!' Hickey was making faint whimpering sounds with eyes and mouth wide open in horror.

The dog snarled fiercely and took a prowling step forward, still ringed with pale, eerie light.

Hickey yelled and ran. Ray followed and the dog went silently after them.

Tony waited until all the noise of running feet and shouting had quite died away. Then he walked slowly home.

Next day Ray and Hickey were waiting as he crossed the playground. They did not touch him or ask him for money. They simply stared at him in a strange sort of way.

'Lucky for you it didn't catch us last night,' Ray muttered.

'You can get into trouble setting dogs on people,' Hickey complained. He sounded feeble.

'No, you can't,' Tony told them, though his mouth was dry. Looking at them, though, he felt braver. Something prompted him to say, 'I've brought him to school with me. Left him outside the gate. He'll stay there all day.' He swallowed, hoping that they were believing him. 'But he'll come soon enough, if I whistle.'

'Set him on me and I'll tell my Dad,' said Hickey, flinching.

'Or the police,' said Ray. They began to slouch away. Then they both broke into a trot.

Days passed and then weeks. Ray and Hickey did not bother him again. He was glad about that. But he was sorry, too. After that moment in the park, neither in his dreams nor at any other time did he see his black dog again.

Looking at the story again

1 In one sentence say what Tony was dreaming about.

2 What did he think had begun his troubles at school?

3 When he and his mother had first come to that town, where had he seen a real dog?

4 What had happened to that dog?

5 Why had Tony not told Miss Williams, the class teacher, about Ray and Hickey?

6 Why was Tony's mother not in a good temper when she got home from work?

7 Why did Tony not want to go across the park to the Shopping Centre?

8 What were Ray and Hickey going to do with the milk?

9 What seems to you the most frightening thing about the dog that Ray and Hickey saw?

10 Why did Ray and Hickey stop bullying Tony?

11 Was Tony right or wrong to lie to Ray and Hickey and say that his dog was waiting at the school gate? Say why you think as you do.

Words

1 What did Tony stare at as he lay in bed? Check your spelling of this word with the spelling in the story.

2 Do you like your own first name? Do you think some first names are more sensible than others? Write down two first names that you like. Don't forget to begin them with a capital letter.

3 'His mother's voice . . . shattered the dream.' Use the word 'shattered' in a sentence of your own.

4 'They began to *slouch* away.' Think of two other

verbs which describe how people walk or move. Then use each one in a sentence of your own.

Writing

1 Did Ray and Hickey realise that the dog they saw was a 'dream' dog or a ghost? Or did they think it was a real dog that belonged to Tony? Write what they might have talked about after they had run away from the dog.

2 Write your own story about a dream. It could be an imaginary one about a dream which came true or it could be the true story of one of your own dreams.

3 Write an account of a shopping trip you went on and enjoyed.

4 Write a story about a dog. It could be one you make up about a dog that is lost or about a dog that frightens people or about a helpful dog. Or, if you have a dog, it could be a true story about your own pet.

5 Write a story about someone going shopping for whom everything goes wrong. He or she might knock over a stack of things in a supermarket or another kind of shop or lose his or her money or all the shopping on a bus.

The Ghost Who Sneezed

Tom Phan, the ghost son of Mr and Mrs Phan, was not well. He missed ghost school that night. When his name was called out: 'Phan Tom' the teacher had to put a 'O' by it in the register. So that night he did not learn how to put his head under his arm in the PE lesson, or how to make clanking chains in the Metalwork lesson.

The trouble was that he had the most dreadful sneezes. One after the other they exploded into the night air. Mrs Phan was sure he was sickening for something. So she took him to see Dr Skull.

They waited several hours in his waiting tomb. There were ghosts with broken bones, ghosts who couldn't shiver properly and ghosts with sore groans. But at last they went in. 'I'm sure Tom has a cold, doctor,' Mrs Phan moaned.

'Ghosts don't get colds,' said Dr Skull. 'You've been mixing too much with the living or watching their TV. Ghosts only get heats. I'll take his temperature. Ah! minus 25 Spookygrade! Quite normal.'

'But these dreadful sneezes, doctor.'

'If he starts coffin,' laughed Dr Skull, 'he'll be all right.'

'Please sound his chest, doctor, he's sneezing and not wheezing.'

'You mothers,' said the doctor. He got out his spectrescope, put it into his ear cavity and listened. 'This is very grave,' he said.

'Oh, doctor!'

'That's a joke.' He grinned till all his teeth rattled. 'Relax. Set your bones at rest. Your son is perfectly deathly. He can go back to school tomorrow.'

'Oh, what a relief, doctor.'

'But no sunlight. That can bring on the sneezes.'

Tom went back to school the next night. But his sneezes got worse. He blew a hole in his haunterchief. He blew the spooks out of the bicycle wheels of his Scottish teacher Mr MacAbre. He was so shaken that he had to drink some spirits to recover. Then, even worse, he blew off one of the heads of the headmaster.

Tom's nose now started to run so Mrs Phan took him to see Dr Bogyman, the consultant at the ghostpital.

'Yes, he has an unhealthy tan,' he said. 'I will give him a bone test.' He put Tom under a white shroud. He shone his green eyes into Tom's. 'Ah,' he said. 'I think I have it. Get me a bunch of flowers from the churchyard,' he said to his assistant.

'Flowers, doctor?' said Mrs Phan. 'Don't say he's going to live!'

'Keep calm, Mrs Phan.'

When the flowers came he put them under Tom's nose. Tom sneezed an almighty sneeze. 'It's hay fever!' shouted the doctor. 'This is the first case I have known in a ghost.'

'Doctor, you're a genie,' said Mrs Phan.

'You son will become famous,' said the doctor.

And so it proved. There was a huge demand from Scottish castles for this famous ghost who sneezed in the summer. Picture two Americans in a four-poster bed:

'George, open the window and let me smell those delicious flowers.'

'Okay, honey.'

'George, did you sneeze?'

'No, honey, I didn't sneeze.'

'There's something in this room that sneezed, George.'

'Well, it wasn't me. I did read in the brochure about this place that they had some spook who sneezed.'

'You didn't tell me, George, that this place was haunted.'

'Atishoo!'

'Oh, George!' The woman jumped right out of her night-dress and ran off screaming.

Tom was given the G.C. for that. Can you guess what the G.C. stands for?

Looking at the story again

1 What was Tom's trouble?

2 Which doctor had a sense of humour?

3 Why does it say 'ear cavity'?

4 Why does the doctor not want Tom in the sunlight?

5 What happened to Mr MacAbre?

6 Why did Mrs Phan take Tom to Dr Bogyman?

7 What did Dr Bogyman do?

8 Why was Tom famous?

9 How do you know the American lady is very frightened?

10 What does G.C. stand for?

Words

1 Think of a name for Tom's ghost school.

2 Explain the joke about the 'coffin'.

3 'Your son is perfectly deathly.' What would *your* doctor say?

4 'haunterchief' – what is our word? Can you spell it properly?

5 'Doctor, you're a genie.' What would *we* say?

Writing

1 What things might Tom learn to do in the drama lesson? Make a list.

2 Make a register of a class of boy and girl ghosts.

3 Write a funny ghost story using one of these titles:
   The Ghost Who Played Tricks
   The Ghost Who Couldn't Moan
   The Ghost With The Wooden Leg

4 Describe two of the ghosts in the waiting tomb of Dr Skull.

5 Write a story called: The Biggest Sneeze in the World.

The Old Schoolmaster

The old man stood wavering on the side of the busy road. Every now and then he would take a tentative step forward, and then a car or lorry would come and he would totter back on to the pavement.

Rahila, Matthew and Julie were walking home from school. They passed the old man. Julie turned to look at him. 'Do you think he wants to be helped across?' she said.

'He'll manage,' said Matthew.

'He's been there all the time we've been walking down the road,' observed Rahila. 'Let's help him.'

'Old people are so funny. He might get cross with us,' said Matthew. 'Come on.'

'No,' said Julie. She went back slowly and hesitated. The old man looked so frail. He was shaking. 'Can I help you?' she asked.

To her relief, the old man smiled. 'That would be very nice,' he said. 'They make these cars and lorries go faster every day. And there's no crossing near here.'

Julie took his arm while the other two held back. It felt so thin; she could feel the bone. He took his first step and Julie realized it would be a slow journey. 'Put your hand up and stop the traffic!' she yelled at Matthew.

Matthew was too shy, but Rahila stepped into the road and held up a lorry. The driver grinned at them. 'Helping Grandad!' he shouted.

'There was a time when I would run across here,'

said the old man.

After what seemed an age they reached the other side. 'That was very kind of you,' said the old man. 'You must come and have a lemonade. I live round the corner.'

Julie remembered what her mother had said about strange men. But there could not possibly be any harm with this old man, and there were three of them. 'Coming?' she asked Rahila.

'I mustn't be late,' said Rahila.

'Mat?'

'I'm going home,' said Mat. He ran off.

'Come on, Rahila,' she urged. She felt that she must see the old man home. She tried to put that feeling into a wink to Rahila.

Rahila seemed to understand.

It was just round the corner but it took a long time. His home was a small red-brick bungalow. The gate hung on one hinge and the garden was overgrown; dark with tall hedges and the branches of fir trees. If the outside was like that what would the inside be like?

She helped him up the step and opened the door. A smart woman met them. She led them into a pleasant room. A fire burned in the grate.

'This is Mrs Jenkins, my home help,' said the old man. 'These children helped me across the road.'

'He will go out on his own,' scolded Mrs Jenkins.

'I've brought them home for a glass of your excellent lemonade.' There was a twinkle in his eye.

The old man made himself comfortable in his high-winged chair. As they sipped their lemonade he told them that he was a retired schoolmaster called Mr Samsworth. He talked with a pleasant chuckle. Julie quickly warmed to him and found herself offering to do the garden for him. 'That would be nice,' said Mrs Jenkins. 'I have no time to do that for him.'

All that spring, summer and autumn Julie and Rahila worked in the garden. Matthew came sometimes. In return Mr Samsworth helped them with their homework. They grew very fond of this kindly old man and he did of them. But there came a day in early winter when Mrs Jenkins met them at the door. Mr Samsworth had died that night. Both Julie and Rahila went home sobbing.

Next day at school they were doing mental arithmetic. Julie hated it; she preferred the calculator. The first one floored her. What were thirteen nines? Then a voice whispered in her ear 'one hundred and seventeen'. She put down this answer. She thought it was the boy behind. The voice, in fact, told her all the answers and she scored twenty out of twenty. She turned to thank the boy behind. But he said that he had not helped her. How could he? He had only got fifteen out of twenty. Julie was puzzled as no other boy was near her. Rahila had also scored twenty out of twenty.

After the class the two girls met. Julie told Rahila about the voice. Rahila said that she had not heard a voice exactly but the answer each time had popped quickly into her mind. They told Matthew after school. He said that he had done a super painting that day and he was not good at art. He said: 'It was as though a hand was guiding mine over the paper.'

Next day during the geography lesson Julie's and Rahila's hands were shooting up all the time to answer questions. 'Well done!' said the teacher. 'At least some people listen to my lessons!'

During the next week Julie, Rahila and Mat got every question right and did excellent practical work. Their teachers were amazed as they were not normally regarded as being very bright.

Going home on the Friday afternoon Julie suddenly stopped. 'Got it,' she said.

'Got what?' asked Rahila.

'That voice that comes to me. I know who it is.'

'Who is it?'

'Mr Samsworth. Why did I not recognize it at first?'

'It's a ghost voice then,' said Rahila.

'But it's not creepy at all,' remarked Julie.

'To think a ghost has touched me,' said Mat.

'Should we tell anybody?' asked Rahila.

'Oh, no,' said Julie. 'We can become top of the class.'

At the end of the term they were all taking home super reports. Rahila stopped and sat on a low wall. 'I've been thinking,' she said. 'It's not right that we should rely on Mr Samsworth to give us all the answers.'

'Why not?' asked Mat. 'It's great.'

'It's making us lazy. We're not using our brains.'

'I've been thinking the same,' said Julie. 'We can't rely on Mr Samsworth all our lives. Though it is nice to be top for a change.'

'I don't like being called a creep,' said Mat.

'We must ask him to stop helping us,' urged Rahila.

'Do you think he will like it?' queried Julie.

'We must do it.'

Next day at school they went into the classroom before the others. 'You say it,' requested Rahila.

'Please, Mr Samsworth,' said Julie trembling, 'don't help us at school because we think we're getting lazy and not learning things for ourselves.'

Nothing happened. The children stood looking around them as though they expected to see something.

'Oh, please,' said Rahila, 'listen to us.'

Then their heads seemed to buzz and they heard a sound like a deep sob. Then nothing.

'He didn't like it,' said Julie.

'It's for our own good,' said Rahila.

'It's a pity,' said Mat.

'He really didn't like it,' repeated Julie.

'Cheer up it's the holidays tomorrow,' said Mat.

Next term it was back to normal. The teachers could not understand why the children could not answer all their questions any more. But the other children stopped calling them swots and creeps.

At the end of the summer term the children were on a coach outing. They were going down a steep hill in Wales. Suddenly the driver was taken ill and he slumped over the wheel. The coach careered down the hill out of control; a big lake was at the bottom. The children screamed.

Julie never knew why but she called out: 'Mr Samsworth!' The wheel of the coach began to steer itself; the engine slowed and the coach came to rest by the lakeside.

The teachers in charge were amazed. But Julie said nothing. That night she had a dream. In it Mr Samsworth came to her. He said that he now had to go a long way away and that he could not help her any more. When she woke up she knew in her heart that it was true.

Looking at the story again

1 How do you know the old man, Mr Samsworth, has been waiting to cross the road for a long time?

2 How do you know that the lorry driver is friendly?

3 Who is the shyest of the three children? What evi-

dence do you have?

4 What was the state of Mr Samsworth's garden?

5 What does a home help do?

6 How does the ghost of Mr Samsworth first help the children?

7 Why is the ghost not frightening?

8 Who is most keen on being helped with school work? Who begins to doubt that they should be helped?

9 How do we know the children upset the ghost?

10 How do we know the ghost still kept an eye on the children after they had sent him away?

Words

1 What words in the first paragraph suggest old age?

2 'people are so funny' – in what ways can you use the word 'funny' in English?

3 Which word best describes the garden?

4 'guiding' – which letter isn't sounded?

5 'amazed' – what other words might describe what the teachers felt?

Writing

1 Describe a grandparent or an old person who lives near you.

2 Write about a strange voice you hear in your bedroom or on the sports field.

3 Describe an overgrown garden.

4 Write about a ghost that could haunt the garden you have described.

5 Write down the reasons (a) *for* being helped by a ghost at school (b) *against* being helped by a ghost at school.

Please Don't Haunt Here

Mr and Mrs Grafton were watching television. Aunty Maud was reading the paper. They all looked up when Tracy and David rushed in.

'Come quick, Dad!' David gabbled.

'There's a man in our garage,' Tracy exclaimed.

'In a big black hat and boots,' David said.

'And a long black coat,' Tracy added.

'He's got a dead white face.'

'And long, bony white hands.'

'And scary eyes.'

'Like little pale-green lights.' They rattled on excitedly.

'Stop pulling me about,' said their father. 'I don't believe a word of it.'

But he went with them. So did Mrs Grafton and Aunty Maud. Sure enough, in the middle of the garage, sitting on a chair, was a man in old-fashioned black clothes. He was smoking a long clay pipe.

'Hey!' said Mr Grafton. 'What are you doing in my garage?'

'Haunting,' said the man.

'Don't talk silly,' said Aunty Maud.

'It's right,' said the man, puffing calmly at his pipe. 'Gallup's the name. Black Jack Gallup. I'm a ghost.'

That made them think. Was he mad or just having a joke?

'Whoever you are, you can't stay here,' said Mrs Grafton at last.

'You're wrong about that,' Black Jack told her.

'I'll get the police,' said Mr Grafton rather weakly.

'Much good that'll do you,' said Black Jack. 'I'll simply disappear if they come – like this.' He became faint and cloud-like and vanished. So did the chair and the pipe.

A thrill of horror ran through them all.

'Has he gone?' Aunty Maud whispered after a while.

'In a manner of speaking,' said Black Jack's voice. He slowly reappeared. 'Course, in another manner of speaking, I'm here all the time.'

'But – why?' asked Tracy.

'Good question,' Black Jack told them. 'I used to haunt the Old Coach House but they've pulled it down to build a motorway. People don't have coaches and horses nowadays,' he went on, as if they didn't know. 'They have cars. I can't have a coach house so I've come to a car house, a garage.'

'Why not just haunt the place where the Old Coach House was?' asked David.

'Out there in the open? Not me. No. You can't haunt properly without four good walls around you most of the time.'

'Why did you have to choose *our* garage?' complained Mrs Grafton.

'There are a lot of much better garages down the street,' hinted Mr Grafton quickly.

'No, there aren't,' Black Jack told him. 'I looked. They're all full of mess and clutter. This one is tidy. I like it here.'

'But Dad's got to get his car in,' Tracy objected.

'Won't bother me,' said Black Jack. 'I'll sit in the back seat. I might go for a drive or two with him.'

'I don't want that,' said Mr Grafton.

'Is that all you do?' asked David.

'What?' said Black Jack.

'Sit about.'

'Bless your heart – no!' Black Jack gave a creaky laugh. 'Most nights I howl and moan. I have a ghostly chain. Sometimes I clank it.'

'Oh Lord!' groaned Mr Grafton.

'You'll disturb the neighbours,' Mrs Grafton said.

'Certainly,' said Black Jack. 'I'm supposed to. That's what ghosts are for. It's a ghost's duty to scare people and I hope I know my duty. Besides moaning, I can turn blue and glow in the dark. Then I can let only bits of myself appear – like just my face or a ghostly claw-like hand. Then there's another good effect where I – '

'Come back in the house, all of you,' Mr Grafton interrupted him. 'We've got to talk about this.'

Tracy wanted to stay and see all the ghost's tricks but her father made her go back into the house with them.

There Aunty Maud said that she would never sleep a wink again, knowing that there was a ghost in the garage. Mrs Grafton said that the neighbours would be furious if he was hooting and howling all night. Mr Grafton said that, if people got to know about it, they would come in crowds just to stare. They'd be trampling all over the garden. Tracy said she thought that the ghost was fun and her mother snapped at her. They were all very upset. Only David thought of something they might do. He suggested that they call in a priest to get rid of Black Jack. No one could think of a better idea. So they all trooped back into the garage to threaten the ghost.

Black Jack said that priests didn't worry him. Priests had been tried on him before and they hadn't worked. They could bring all the priests they wanted. But – if they did – he would start haunting the house as well.

They didn't like the thought of that at all so they decided to forget about a priest.

Black Jack did give them a lot of trouble. His moans kept them and the neighbours awake. The neighbours all complained. Mr Wilson next door said that he would 'have the law on' Mr Grafton. The milkman stopped calling. He said the ghost had come 'shimmering' out of the garage at him early one morning. It had stood at the door grinning. Then it had made grabbing movements with its hands at him and he had run away.

Other people, probably because Tracy talked about nothing else at school, heard about the ghost and came to see. Most evenings when it grew dark a crowd gathered in the garden, in spite of all Mr Grafton's efforts to stop them, and stood peering into the garage. Sometimes they saw Black Jack and sometimes they didn't. Some of the cheeky ones who hadn't seen Black Jack knocked on the door to complain and to ask Mr Grafton if he couldn't 'stir the ghost up a bit' so that he became visible. Some of those who had seen Black Jack knocked on the door to complain, too. They said he had scared the life out of them and 'it shouldn't be allowed'. They all tramped over the front garden, breaking down Mr Grafton's favourite roses and stamping the flowers flat.

The police complained, too. They said that all the cars with the people in them coming to see the ghost were causing serious parking difficulties in the area. They asked Mr Grafton what he was going to do about it. He said that it was their problem and they all had a long and noisy argument on the front doorstep.

Mr Grafton had another quarrel with the television people. They came to film the ghost for a news item. They waited for over an hour but Black Jack did not appear. The producer asked Mr Grafton in a sneering sort of way if there really was a ghost at all. This was just as the television van was backing into the Grafton's drive to turn round and go away. It bumped Mr Grafton's car and Mr Grafton lost his temper. After the television people had gone Mr and Mrs Grafton had another row about Mr Grafton's bad language and shouting for all the street to hear.

One evening Mr Grafton was in the front room looking gloomily out of the window at the crowd jostling about in front of his garage. He had given up asking them not to stand on his car roof. Aunty Maud who was reading the paper suddenly said, 'What a pity!'

'It's more than a pity,' said Mr Grafton. 'It's a downright liberty!'

Then Aunty Maud explained that she had not meant the ghost but Harker Hall. It was a big house in the country open to visitors. She had been there a couple of times and enjoyed it. Now – the newspaper said – it was having to close down and be sold for lack of money. Not enough people were going to see it.

'I'll bet it doesn't have a ghost,' grumbled Mr Grafton.

'Dad!' said David. 'I've got an idea.'

When he explained his plan, there was great excitement. Mr Grafton rang the owner of Harker Hall, a Sir Sidney Barton-Fish, at once and Sir Sidney came over right away. They forced their way through the crowd outside the garage. This was larger than usual since Black Jack had not only appeared but was putting on some special effects.

'Spendid!' said Sir Sidney as soon as he saw Black Jack. 'Just the thing.' He told Jack what they wanted and asked. 'How about it, old man?'

Black Jack did not seem too keen at first. Mr Grafton was in despair.

'Superb old coach house at my place,' urged Sir Sidney. 'Wouldn't hurt you just to take a look.'

Jack, seemingly quite impressed by Sir Sidney, admitted that he might do that and disappeared. The crowd drifted sulkily away, making remarks and breaking down some more of the Graftons' hedge. Sir Sidney and the Graftons waited in the garage for what seemed a long time. Mr Grafton paced up and down, biting his nails.

When Jack reappeared he said shortly, 'I'll do it.'

'Thank God!' Mr Grafton exclaimed.

'And I dropped in on a mate of mine,' Jack went on, ignoring him. 'He's the Headless Horseman of Hangman Hill. He drives a coach and horses. He says he'll let me borrow them four nights a week. He's getting old and finds his kind of haunting gets tiring. I could drive them out of your coach house, striking terror into the hearts of all who see me. How about it?'

'Splendid!' said Sir Sidney. 'A stroke of genius!'

'I know,' said Jack.

He left the Graftons' garage that night. Things went very well for everybody. People very soon left the Graftons alone but huge crowds began to flock from all over Britain to Harker Hall to see the ghostly coachman and his coach and horses. Sir Sidney's bank balance did so well out of it that he gave Mr Grafton money to have his car re-sprayed and his garden done with enough over for the Graftons to have a good holiday.

One evening that summer, the Graftons visited

Harker Hall. Like the rest of the crowd there, they shuddered with fear as the coach doors swung silently open. Six ghastly horses drew a ghostly coach, horribly lit-up from inside. Jack, of course, was driving. As the coach drifted soundlessly past the Graftons and just before it vanished, Jack winked at them and lifted a thumb.

'He seems happy at Harker Hall,' said Mrs Grafton afterwards when Mr Grafton had parked in the drive outside their house to let them all out of the car.

'Best place for him,' said Aunty Maud.

'I think so,' said Mr Grafton.

They all closed the car doors behind them and began to walk to the front door. Smiling happily, he drove into his clean, tidy and quite empty garage.

Looking at the story again

1 Why did Tracy and David want their father to go with them to the garage?

2 What did they all see in the garage?

3 What did Black Jack do when Mr Grafton said he would get the police?

4 Where had Black Jack haunted before?

5 Why could he not still haunt there?

6 How did Mr Grafton feel about having Black Jack with him in his car?

7 What did Black Jack say he would do if they brought a priest to get rid of him?

8 Which of the neighbours complained first about the ghost?

9 Why did the milkman stop calling?

10 What happened to the Graftons' garden and why did it happen?

11 Who found out that Harker Hall was going to be sold?

12 Who got a good idea from that piece of news and what was the idea?

13 What good idea did Black Jack have to improve his haunting of Harker Hall?

14 How did Sir Sidney repay the Graftons?

15 How did Mr Grafton feel about the solution to the problem?

Words

1 'old-fashioned'; 'calmly'; 'disappear'; 'visible'. Write one word *opposite* in meaning to each of these.

2 When he is talking to Aunt Maud, Mr Grafton says that something is a 'downright liberty!' Explain in your own words what he means.

3 What is a 'bank balance'?

4 Use the word 'jostling' in a sentence of your own to show its meaning.

Writing

1 A strange visitor comes to see you one day. Is he or she a long-lost relative? Is the visitor an alien from space? A ghost? Why has the visitor come to your house? Write the story.

2 What sort of entertainment might there be at Harker Hall? Would there be animals to see? Might there be a small fairground? Could you ride on a train? Either write down a description of what you might find to do on a day out at Harker Hall *or*, if you have ever visited a big house in the country, write a description of what you saw and did.

3 What is the most interesting or most unusual prog-

ramme you have ever seen on television? Write about it.

4 Black Jack Gallup puts on some 'special effects' for the crowd at the door of the garage. Write about what you might see, if you were one of the crowd.

5 Mr Grafton is not a lucky man and things often go wrong for him. Write about what happens when he and his family decide to decorate a room or to do the gardening together.

6 Black Jack, the ghost, goes to see another ghost, The Headless Horseman of Hangman Hill, to borrow his coach and horses. Was it easy for Black Jack to persuade the Headless Horseman to lend him the coach? Write down what the two might have talked about when they met.

The House On The Moor

'You're a fool!' Clare snapped.

'No, I'm not,' Tim, her brother, said.

Jill said nothing. She was cold and scared. It was getting dark. Over the moors around them the fog was growing thicker.

'They'll be looking for us by now,' Tim said.

'How can they be looking for us?' Clare argued angrily. 'They don't know where we've gone.'

'Let's shout again,' Tim suggested.

'All right,' Clare agreed.

They called out. Jill joined in.

'Can anyone hear us?'

'Help! We're lost!'

'Over here!'

When they stopped, it felt even more lonely. All they could hear was the sound of a stream in the distance.

'They'll find us,' Tim said.

'Will they?' Clare grumbled.

'Which way shall we go now?' Jill asked. Neither of them answered her. She felt very cold. She wished she had never left home.

She was staying with Tim and Clare. For a holiday, early in the year, their parents had rented a cottage. It belonged to a farmer called Mr Clark and it was on the edge of the moors. Clare's Mum and Dad had told them not to go wandering off. Tim, though, had wanted to go exploring. That afternoon they had set off. They hadn't, of course, said

anything to Tim and Clare's Mum and Dad.

It had been all right at first. It had been a cool, windy day. There were clouds in the sky but it was sunny, too. Then the wind had dropped and the clouds had slowly covered all the sky. It got colder and a mist began to creep across the moors. Then they found they were lost. They had been over so many hills and down so many valleys that none of them knew the way back.

'We could be out here all night,' Clare said.

'We can't be.' Tim shivered. 'We'll freeze.'

'Well – which way do we go?' Jill repeated. They looked at each other, then at the empty moors around them.

'It's – ghostly,' said Clare.

'It'll be worse after dark,' Tim half-whispered.

'Come on,' Jill told them. 'Let's try this way.' She walked on and the others followed her up the hill. They reached the top but there was still nothing to see but fog and brown heather.

'They'll never find us.' Clare's voice shook.

'We'd better keep moving,' Tim said grimly.

He walked on, Clare slowly followed and Jill went last. Her legs were very tired. She was hungry.

Down in the bottom of the next valley they could not see the tops of the hills on either side. The fog hid them. Clare slumped down on a rock.

'I'm so tired,' she whimpered. 'So cold. We'll never get home.' She started to cry. Jill and Tim looked at her. They were too tired to think of anything to say.

'Now then! What's all this about?' The sudden harsh voice made them all jump. The old woman seemed to have come up out of the ground. She had grey hair, pulled tightly back in a knot. Her mouth was thin and her face was wrinkled. She wore a long black dress with a grey shawl over her shoulders.

'We're lost,' Tim told her.

'Thought as much. Town children, eh? Well!' She stared at them rather bad-temperedly, Jill thought. 'You'd best come with me.'

The old woman set off so quickly that they had to hurry to keep up with her. She led them up a track out of the valley, over the hill and down the other side. They came to a farm.

Jill rubbed her eyes. Tiredness was making it hard for her to see things clearly. The house and the other buildings round it seemed dim, though it was not yet all that dark.

'Come in, come in,' the old woman ordered. 'Don't stand about in the yard.'

Inside the house it was really dark. A small fire burned in the hearth. The old woman did not put any lights on. All the furniture looked very old. There was a rag rug on the stone floor.

'Here!' Jill found the old woman was offering her milk in a thick cup and a slice of bread. She felt strange, as if she were half-asleep. Eating the bread did not make her feel less hungry and she was still thirsty after drinking the milk. No one spoke. The old woman sat by the fire, staring at the three of them. In the dark her face was a pale blur, almost white.

When she spoke, it made them all jump again.

'They'll be looking for you,' she said in that harsh voice. 'They'll be coming by way of Bleakmile Lane. Come with me.'

She got up quickly and disappeared through the door. Jill put her cup down and went after her, followed by the other two. She led them down the farmtrack and out into a narrow lane, walking so fast that it was hard to keep up with her.

'Where are we going?' Tim called.

She did not answer. Her black dress seemed part of the gathering darkness. Her grey hair and grey shawl wavered ahead of them like smoke. They came to a wider road and she stopped.

'Wait!' she ordered in her rough voice but she hardly needed to tell them. They could all hear the approaching car. When its lights lit up the road and the hedges on either side, they called out and waved. It stopped. It was Mr Clark's Land Rover. Clare's parents got out.

'Where the devil have you been?' Clare's father demanded but both he and Clare's mother were too relieved to be really angry. Tim explained what had happened and told them about the old woman.

'She's – where has she gone?' He looked up and down the road. She had vanished.

'What did she look like?' Mr Clark asked. Tim told him.

'And where did you say she took you?'

'Up there.' Tim pointed.

'Hm. Very odd,' said Mr Clark. 'Let's have a look.'

They all got into the Land Rover and went back the way they had come. When they stopped at the top of the farmtrack and got out, it was eerie. In the headlights they could see only ruined walls and scattered stones. A broken chimney pointed up out of the roofless walls to the sky.

'But there was a farm here!' Clare gasped. 'We went in.'

'You met Mrs Lucas,' Mr Clark told them. 'There are stories about her in these parts. She farmed up here with her son, Jack, fifty or sixty years ago. She was a bitter, hard woman and a slave-driver to Jack. One night of storm and snow she sent him out to look for sheep. He never came back. When they found him he had frozen to death. She didn't live long after that and the farm fell into ruin. People say that she was sorry for what she had done to Jack. Now, they say, to make up for what she did, she sometimes helps lost travellers.'

'You mean – we saw a ghost?' Tim whispered.

'A friendly one,' said Mr Clark.

A small cold breeze played with Jill's hair for a moment. She shivered and got quickly into the back of the Land Rover. It was warmer in there. It felt safe but she wondered whether the thin, white-faced figure of Mrs Lucas would walk through her dreams that night. A quick clapping call broke the silence around them for a second or two. She shivered again. She hoped it was a late bird's cry. But then again – it could have been an old woman's harsh laughter sounding faintly from far away.

Looking at the story again

1 At the beginning of the story, why were the children scared?

2 Why would their parents not be looking for them?

3 Which of the children had decided to go exploring?

4 Whom did they suddenly meet?

5 What did that person look like?

6 Where did she take the children?

7 What was it like inside the farmhouse?

8 What was strange about the milk that Jill drank and the bread she ate?

9 When they left the farm where did the old woman take the children?

10 Who was Mr Clark?

11 What happened to the old woman after the children were found?

12 When they got to the farm again what did it look like?

13 What was the name of the old woman?

14 What was the name of her son and what happened to him?

15 Why, according to some people, does the old woman help lost travellers?

16 What – right at the end of the story – does Jill think she might have heard?

Words

1 Write out the first question in the story. Don't forget the question mark.

2 'When they stopped, it felt even more lonely.' Complete the following sentences, using your own words:

When the bus stopped. . .

When she saw me. . .

When I go on my holidays. . .

3 'Tiredness' – think of three other words ending in 'ness' and use each one in a sentence of your own.

Writing

1 Write your own story about a group of children lost in a lonely place in bad weather. It need not have a ghost in it.

2 Describe what you think the kitchen of an old-fashioned farmhouse would look like. Use the picture and some of the description in the story to help you.

3 Jill tells her friends about meeting the old woman. Do they all believe her or do some of them think she is making it up? Write down the kind of conversation they might have.

4 Write a story about a boy or girl who is ill-treated by the grown-up person or persons he or she lives with. It could be a story about today or about many years ago. Make it end happily.

5 Write about being out alone in the country in the dark or in fog. You could write this as a story or as a poem.

The Ghostly Computer

'I hate funerals,' said Samantha. 'I shall never go to one again!'

'Yes, you will,' said her friend Helen.

'No, I won't!'

'Yes, you will.'

'I won't. It was horrible!'

'You'll go to your own, you silly.'

'This is no day for jokes,' insisted Samantha.

Indeed it was not a day for jokes. Samantha's best friend had just been buried. Tina had forgotten her Green Cross Code. She had not used the crossing near the school and had been knocked down by a lorry.

Back at the school their teacher, Miss Wade, knew it would be a difficult day and it would be hard to make the children work. Instead she had invented a new game for the computer: it was called Jungle Crossing. You had to go through the jungle avoiding lions, gorillas, soldier ants and swamps. It had taken her all week to write the program for the game.

Soon there were oohs and aahs in the classroom as the children forgot about the funeral and enjoyed the new game. But Samantha sat away from it all at the back of the class. Miss Wade went to her. 'Come on, Samantha, have just one game.'

'I don't want to, Miss. It's not a day for games.'

But the children were having so much fun that Samantha wandered up to watch and finally sat

down at the keyboard. She typed in her name. 'Hello, Samantha,' it said, 'would you like to play Jungle Crossing?' Samantha typed in 'Yes'. But instead of the jungle display appearing a number flashed on the VDU. It was 271084.

Miss Wade looked puzzled. There must be a bug in the program. Yet it had been all right for the other children. She pressed a key and the number disappeared. She pressed another and the jungle display came back. Samantha escaped the lions and the gorillas but just as she reached the soldier ants another number appeared: 216. Miss Wade was even more puzzled. She set up the game again but after Samantha had avoided the final obstacle a letter and a number flashed on the VDU: D6. It flashed several times and then disappeared.

'You try, Helen,' said Miss Wade.

Helen played and the game went through perfectly.

Miss Wade took her program home that weekend and looked for bugs in it. But she could find none. It just went against the logic for computers that a game should be different when one person played it. The children played for a lesson on the Monday. It was right every time except when Samantha played and then the strange numbers appeared. They were always the same.

On Tuesday, walking home with Helen, Samantha said, 'I feel as though somebody is trying to get a message to me.'

Helen stopped. 'That's it!' she exclaimed. 'Someone is trying to tell you something through the computer.'

'But who?'

'Yes, who?'

'Now I think of it, I keep seeing Tina in my mind

but I thought that was because I loved her so.'

'We must tell Miss Wade.'

The children rushed back to school.

'You're just being fanciful,' she said to calm them. But she did not think that. She knew something was very odd. Why should 271084, 216 and D6 flash on the VDU? There was no logical reason. These numbers were not in the program.

'We've got to work out the numbers,' said Helen.

'Well, you're the brain-box,' Samantha told her.

'I'll write to the computer makers,' said Miss Wade.

Helen had a letter the next morning. It was dated 25/10/84. The cornflake packet was over the '25' and the '10/84' part clicked in her mind. It was the same as the computer. They had been thinking of it as a whole number but it could be the date: the 27th of October 1984. That was tomorrow!

She must tell Samantha. She must hurry. She glanced at her watch: 8.16. Another flash of inspiration came to her. '216' could be a time. Sixteen minutes past two.

She ran to the school to tell Samantha and Miss Wade. She burst into the classroom to find them both there. 'It's a date and a time. She must be warning us of something that is going to happen tomorrow. But where?'

'Sit down, Helen, and explain,' said Miss Wade.

Helen told her her theory. 'You're being fanciful again,' she said. But now she shared the children's fears. She had told no other teacher but now she went to the headteacher.

'The idea of a computer with children, Miss Wade, is to teach them something, not develop hysteria. Now go back and calm down the class.'

But the class would not be calmed. 'I have seen D6

52

in a classroom recently,' said Helen.

Despite Miss Wade asking them not to the whole class went round the school at break. They found nothing. But just as they were beginning the next lesson Kishan rushed in. 'I've got it!' he yelled. 'I've seen it. D6 is a square on the grid of the town map. And in the square is the school. In fact the only building in the square is this school as the rest is playing fields and parks!'

'That's it!' shouted Helen. 'Something is going to happen to the school.'

'Why does D6 *flash*?' asked Samantha.

'The school is going to catch fire,' said Helen. The class screamed. Miss Wade could not calm them down. She had to fetch the headteacher.

He came and lectured them for a quarter of an hour about behaviour and hysteria. But they still did not settle. Samantha stood up. 'Please, Mr Samson, I feel Tina is trying to tell us that something is going to happen to the school. We must have a day off tomorrow.'

'Ah, that's your trick,' said Mr Samson.

'No, I didn't mean it like that. Tina is warning us.'

'Then why does she have to make it a riddle?' asked Mr Samson. 'Why is there no clear message?'

'Tina was dyslexic,' said Helen. 'She did not like words.'

Kishan stood up. 'I'm not coming in tomorrow,' he said. Others agreed with him. The head could see that he was losing control.

'Very well,' he said. 'I'll tell you what I'll do. We'll hold a fire practice at two o'clock tomorrow. No harm can come to anyone in the playground.'

Little work was done next day. Several agitated parents came to see the head. He was glad when two o'clock came and he could get this nonsense over. He rang the fire bell.

The staff shouted at the children not to run, to stop talking and to treat it as a normal fire practice. But the children did not line up. They gathered in groups round those pupils with watches. Then as it neared 2:16 there was an awesome silence.

It was rent by a terrific explosion. The roof of Samantha's classroom fell in. The children screamed and ducked. The head ran for the phone.

There were a few scratches from the flying glass but no one was badly hurt. It was a gas explosion. The children gathered round Samantha and Helen to thank them. 'You should thank Tina,' Samantha said.

'And the ghostly computer,' said Helen.

Looking at the story again

1 What takes the children's mind off the funeral?
2 Who is the last to play?
3 What happens when Samantha plays?
4 What happens when Helen plays?
5 What can't Miss Wade understand?
6 What do the children rush back to school for?
7 Who discovers the first clue?
8 What is the headteacher's attitude to Miss Wade's fears?
9 What does the headteacher finally decide to do?
10 What happens as 2:16 approaches?

Words

1 What is a computer bug? Is it alive?
2 What does VDU stand for?
3 'fanciful' – write down three other words that end in 'ful'.

4 If you get very excited you might be said to be suffering from 'hy___'.

5 Complete this expression which describes an awesome silence: 'you could hear a ___ ___'.

Writing

1 What main things do you remember about The Green Cross Code?

2 Describe the best computer game you ever played.

3 Write two sentences to describe a big explosion.

4 Copy out your school fire drill in your best handwriting.

5 Write a play in which a computer helps you and your friends to find some treasure.

The Midnight Horses

Dew soaked into their shoes and buttercups stained their white socks. A disturbed lark suddenly zigzagged into the blue haze of the sky. Rachel jumped. 'Oh!' she gasped.

'It's only a bird,' said her younger sister Sheila.

Rachel took her hand. She turned sharp left to avoid a cow ripping up the grass. She would feel happier when they had reached the gate out of its curious gaze.

'You don't like it here,' accused the younger girl.

'No, I don't. It's either boiling hot or soaking with rain. Look at my shoes!'

'That's dew, silly, not rain.'

'There's mud everywhere all the time. And I don't like the smells.'

'Better than petrol fumes. I love the country. I don't ever want to go back to the town again. I want to live and die here.'

'What a thing to say.' She just did not understand her sister sometimes. She lived in a world which was not hers. 'You've got to go back to the home the day after tomorrow,' she said.

'I hate the home. It's like a prison. Here you can feel free. Whee!' She raised her arms like an aeroplane. 'Do you think there is a land at the end of the wind?'

Rachel ignored the daft question. 'Well, I shall be glad to get back. There are no discos here, no cinema, no ice-skating – nothing. Just fields of nothing.' She beheaded a dandelion with her stick.

They reached the gate. Rachel felt relieved since the cow was still staring at her.

'I have a secret,' said Sheila.

'What?'

'I'm not telling.'

'There's nothing to have secrets about in the country.'

'I have a big secret.'

'I bet it's a silly one. I know your secrets.'

'No, this is the biggest secret ever.'

'Tell me.'

'I'll tell you tonight. Come on, I'll race you back to the camp.'

'I'm not running. It's dangerous in all this long grass.'

'Oh, come on.'

Sheila ran back to the tents. Rachel followed slowly, eyes on the ground. She was annoyed about the secret.

They had snuggled into their sleeping bags. 'What is this secret then?' asked Rachel.

'I'll tell you when the camp is asleep,' Sheila whispered.

'I don't want to know then. Don't you dare wake me up.' She did not like lying awake in the country. There were noises. Strange hootings and rustlings. She was sure the rustlings were rats. But worse than that were the country stories of things in the field at night. An old lady who looked like a witch had told them that they should never have been camping in those fields. When asked why, she had tapped her nose and said: 'I don't want to talk about the things. It is bad luck.'

Rachel turned on her side and shut her eyes tight.

The next thing she knew there was a whisper in

her ear. 'Come on, it's time.'

'What?'

'It's time to go for the secret.'

'Go where?'

'Into the big field by the brook.'

'I'm not going into the big field at this time of night.'

'I'll go on my own then.'

'You can't.'

'I've been for the past two nights.'

'What is it?'

'Horses.'

'Horses!' Getting up in the middle of the night to see horses. Her sister was potty.

'These are special horses. You'll see.' She was half out of the tent.

Her mother, when the family had split up, had charged her always to look after her sister. She felt compelled to get out of the warm bed and see what she was up to. She pulled her parka over her pyjamas and slipped on her shoes.

A full moon shone outside, casting frightening shadows from the trees. All was strangely still. Not an owl or a rustling. She could see her sister halfway across the field. She dare not call out for fear of waking the house mother so she stumbled after her across tufts of grass.

Sheila was by the gate. 'Come on,' she said, 'into this tree.'

'This really is most silly. I hate tree climbing. You could break your neck.'

'It's best up the tree. Come on.'

She felt she must save her sister from falling so she climbed. The moon gave them enough light. Sheila stopped on a branch eight feet from the ground.

'This really is so silly. There, I've torn my pyjamas

and I've lost a shoe.'

'Sh! It's nearly midnight. Watch!'

'Watch what?'

'Over there.'

A faint drumming sound could be heard like rain on a roof.

'What is it? I'm frightened, Sheila.'

'There's nothing to be frightened of. Look!'

Three magnificent white horses suddenly appeared, tossing their heads and snorting. Each had a long mane and tail. They looked completely wild. They seemed to move like a slow-motion film for at no time was one of their legs on the ground.

'Aren't they magnificent?'

'You know I hate horses. We must get back to the camp!'

'Don't frighten them.'

The horses ran round the field in a long curve. Then they turned.

'They're coming this way,' said Rachel. Her heart raced.

'They always do,' said Sheila in a matter of fact way.

'Oh, no! Oh, no!'

The horses came slowly yet quickly to the tree. They jostled to rub their long coats against the trunk. They were right underneath them.

'I'm going to ride one,' said Sheila.

'No!'

'I must. I must. I must!'

'No!'

'Let me go. I must ride one!'

The bigger girl clung on to the shoulder of the younger. It needed all her strength to stop overbalancing. But a terrible foreboding gave her extra power to restrain her sister. Then to her relief the horses galloped off. A faint drumming and they were gone.

'Why didn't you let me?'

'I didn't let you because you could kill yourself, you young fool.'

'I wish I had never let you come.'

'Come on back to the tents at once.'

'You spoil-sport.'

'You must promise me not to come here tomorrow night.'

'I must see them again. I can't go back to town without.'

'I order you.'

'You're not ordering me!'

They stumbled back through the darkness arguing. The moon was now cloud-covered.

Next day Rachel saw the house mother.

'No, we cannot go back, dear. Not till tomorrow. The coach will not be here till then.'

'But I hate the country.'

'I know you do, dear. But the others are enjoying it so much, especially your sister. Be patient, there's a good girl.'

'But there are things here. In these fields at night.'

'You've been listening to the country folk. You're quite safe. Now run along.'

'But I've seen them.'

'Just dreams, dear. Just dreams.' It was such a pity she was not enjoying the holiday.

Rachel would not go to sleep that night. She would hold on to Sheila. She would make sure she went nowhere near that field and tree. She would not go to sleep. But she did.

She woke in a sweat, dreaming of being trampled by white horses. She felt for her sister. She was not there.

With a cry she ran out of the tent. In her mind she could see Sheila riding across the field on the back of a white horse. The phantom horses. The horses that did not smell.

The house mother was roused by the cry. She ran after Rachel. By this time Rachel was at the tree. Sheila was not there. 'The horses!' she yelled. 'Sheila's been taken by the horses.'

'We'll find your sister,' comforted the house mother. 'I'll wake the camp. In this moonlight we'll soon spot her.'

They found her in a ditch at the end of the field. She had a smile on her face. 'I rode the horses,' she said.

'You've been sleep-walking, dear,' said the house mother.

'No, I rode the horses and it was like heaven.'

'Come on, I'll carry you. I think you've had a bit of a bump on the head.'

After that Rachel could never enter Sheila's world. When they left the home when Sheila was old enough they moved into a flat. One day when Rachel came home from work she found a note. It just said: 'Gone to the country'. She never saw her again after that.

Looking at the story again

1 Who does not like the countryside?

2 What is the daft question Sheila asks?

3 Who is afraid of cows?

4 What did the old lady look like?

5 What has Sheila been doing for the past two nights?

6 Why does Rachel get up to follow her sister in the night?

7 Why did the moon make it seem frightening?
8 What is the first sign of the midnight horses?
9 What clues are there that the horses are not real?
10 Do you think Sheila rode the horses? Why?

Words

1 'dandelion' – write down five other wild flowers.
2 'relieved' – what other words do you know with 'ie' in them?
3 What words would you use to describe a galloping horse?
4 'overbalancing' – write down three words that begin with 'over'.

Writing

1 Turn the scene when the girls see the horses into an unrhymed poem.
2 Write about walking in the rain.
3 Something in your area is killing pets. Is it an animal escaped from a safari park or is there something ghostly about it? Write a report for your local newspaper.
4 Put down the good things (a) about the town (b) about the country.
5 Write the story of what happens to Sheila.

Ghost Spray

Susan knew she was going to be sorry but her feet took her up the steps and into the library. One of the shelves she knew very well. Again, something like black magic drew her towards it. One of the books on the shelf was new to her. *Things in the Night* it said on the spine.

Susan looked quickly away. She was not going to read any more ghost stories. She was finished with all that. She wanted a book about animals. She was very interested in animals now, she told herself.

Her eyes, though, returned to *Things in the Night*. It wouldn't hurt just to look at the picture on the cover. She took the book from the shelf. The cover, all blues and greens, showed a woman with streaming hair and terrified eyes, running away from something. She was in a graveyard. It was night time and it was misty.

As though they didn't belong to her, Susan's fingers opened the book. A title, 'Lost Hearts' caught her eye. She couldn't help herself. She took the book into the Children's Section of the library, found a seat and began to read.

'Five minutes to closing time, dear.' The voice of the librarian made Susan nearly jump out of her skin. She looked up but the librarian had moved on. Quickly Susan finished the story, shut the book, put it gently on a table and set off home.

It had been a horrible story. She hadn't been able to stop herself reading it but it had been horrible –

terrifying. That was the trouble. Susan enjoyed reading ghost stories, the more terrifying the better. She couldn't keep away from them.

What she didn't enjoy was going to bed after she had read them. She didn't have nightmares; she didn't even remember much of the ghost stories she had read. It was the ghosts she felt she was just about to meet that scared her nearly to death. They weren't ghosts of people. They were – Things. Sometimes you heard them coming. They whispered outside the window or they creaked up the stairs. Sometimes you almost saw them. They were little flickerings or clots of shadow in the almost dark of the bedroom. When you looked directly at them, they kept very still. Sometimes you almost felt the ghostly Things. Susan was sure there was a Thing under her bed. One night it was going to arch its back just as Susan was dropping off to sleep and lift the mattress with Susan on it.

Every night it seemed hours before she grew too tired to be afraid any longer and went to sleep.

Her mother found out and told Susan not to be silly. Then she agreed to leave the light outside Susan's bedroom on all night. Then her mother banned all books of ghost stories from the house and told Susan to read something more 'healthy'. The library, though, was on the way home for Susan. Sometimes she couldn't stop herself from going in.

Then she went to stay for a week with her Aunty Mary and Uncle Alan. She hadn't seen them for a long time or stayed in their house before. Things got much worse.

For one thing, Uncle Alan had a lot of books. Among them was a set of five thick volumes called, *The World's Thousand Best Ghost Stories*. Susan could not help just glancing at a few. Then she read some.

The first was about a ghost animal. The second was about a hand that crept about the house. Another was about a picture with a Thing in it. Each time you looked at the picture, the Thing had moved.

Besides that, the house that Aunty Mary and Uncle Alan lived in was quite old. At night it was full of rustlings and shufflings and creakings. Things scraped at or brushed against the window panes of Susan's bedroom. A wind – or some Thing – kept faintly wailing in a chimney. And the Thing from under Susan's bed at home had come with her. It was lurking, there under Susan's bed in Aunty Mary and Uncle Alan's house, just waiting for Susan to put the light out.

So, when Aunty Mary and Uncle Alan came up-stairs they found Susan sitting up in bed with her light still on. They were quite kind and not angry but she had to explain. She felt silly but, to her surprise, Uncle Alan seemed to understand.

He said that he, too, had often been bothered with ghosts. Then he had met a very wise old man, a ghost-hunter. He had given Uncle Alan a special preparation which always got rid of ghosts. It never failed. Uncle Alan had used it and never had any trouble with ghosts since.

'What is it?' asked Susan.

'You'll see,' said Uncle Alan and went downstairs. Aunty Mary plumped up Susan's pillow and straightened the bedclothes.

'I'll get you some warm milk,' she said and she left, too.

They were both gone for some time. Aunty Mary came back first and Susan drank her milk. Then Uncle Alan came in and put what he was carrying into Susan's hand. It was an aerosol spray can. It did not have a proper label. Round the can was a sheet of red paper. On the paper, in green and ornamental lettering, it said 'Ghost Spray'. Susan pressed the knob on the top of the can. Nothing came out.

'It's empty,' she said.

'It's full,' said Uncle Alan. 'You don't see it or hear it or smell it because it's ghost spray. Only ghosts can feel it. It works and never needs re-filling. Try it.'

He looked at her with a serious face. Then he nodded and he and Aunty Mary left the room, switching off the light. Susan was left in the darkness, clutching her can.

At first she was half-afraid to try it just in case, for her, it wasn't going to work. Then she pointed it at the flickering Things in the corners of the room and pressed the knob. They became – just shadows. She sprayed the window and the noises there became only the sound of the wind in the trees outside. She sprayed towards the door and the shufflings and rustlings beyond it became merely sounds of old woodwork cooling down. Finally, she got all her courage together, dropped her hand over the side of the bed, gave two quick squirts under the bed and pulled her hand swiftly back. The Thing under the bed vanished immediately. She was sure of it.

She hardly had time to think much about the mysterious and magical spray. She was so relieved she fell asleep at once.

When her stay at Aunty Mary's was over and she went home again, she took the Ghost Spray with her. Then, quite soon, she stopped using it much. It was so very good at making all the ghosts disappear. After a time she felt that, with her Ghost Spray, the poor old ghosts were much more frightened of her than she was of them.

Looking at the story again

1 What was the new book on the library shelf called?
2 What was the picture on the cover?
3 Which of the stories in the book did Susan read?
4 Why do you think Susan jumped when the librarian spoke to her?
5 What did Susan *not* enjoy about ghost stories?
6 Which Thing did Susan seem most afraid of?
7 How did her mother try to help Susan to get to sleep at night?
8 Whom did Susan go to stay with?
9 Which book of her uncle's interested Susan the most?
10 Why was Susan's light still on when her uncle and aunt came to bed?
11 What did her Aunty Mary do to help Susan sleep?
12 What did her Uncle Alan give Susan?
13 What was her uncle's explanation when Susan said that the thing seemed empty?
14 What happened when she used it on the Things in the corner of her room?
15 Why did Susan stop using the spray much after a time?

Words

1 'whisper'; 'creak' – the sounds of these two words seem to imitate the sounds they describe. Think of three other words that imitate sounds and use each one in a sentence of your own.
2 How do you feel if something makes you 'nearly jump out of your skin'?
3 There is another word for 'book' in the story. It is in the description of Uncle Alan's collection of books. Find the word and write it down.

4 'She was so relieved she fell asleep at once.' Complete the following sentences using your own words:

   They were so happy that. . .

   She was so angry that. . .

   The lost dog was so friendly that. . .

5 'He had given Uncle Alan a special *preparation* which always got rid of ghosts.' Write out that sentence using another word meaning almost the same as 'preparation'.

Writing

1 Write a short account of the most frightening story you have ever read.

2 What might the Things that Susan imagined have looked like? Write a short description of one of them.

3 One day you find something ordinary like a pen, or a cup, or even an old bike. You might like to pick some other object. Then you find that it can perform a kind of magic. What can it do and what happens when you use it? Write the story.

4 Do you have any good advice to a person who can't sleep? If so, make a list of some of the things you might advise him or her to do to help.

5 You are alone in the house one night and you hear a mysterious noise. You go to find out what it is. Is it something not very important like a window banging in the wind or a bird or a cat that has got in? Or is it something more serious? Write about what happens.

The River

Jane and her family moved to a house in the country. At first the different night noises out there, the wind, the screech of owls, the rushing river, kept them awake. Then all of them, except Jane, got used to the sounds. Jane never got used to the river. It fascinated her.

There was a lane at the front of the house. Beyond that, a small field sloped down to the river. Jane's bedroom overlooked the field. Most nights before she went to sleep she heard the water flowing. It was only in summer when the river was low that it sounded faint and far away.

Jane was the odd one out in the family. Her mother and father both worked in town. They were brisk, efficient people. So was Martin, Jane's brother. He was four years older than Jane and doing very well at school. Things never went wrong for him as they did for Jane. He was like his parents. Jane was different. She was dreamy and untidy and all three of them often had to tell her about it.

Whenever she had been in trouble, though, a walk by the river afterwards always made things seem better. She would walk up the lane to the old, rickety bridge and hang over its rail watching the brown water swirl past its posts. Then she would make her way back to the house along the bank. She would stoop under overhanging trees, splash through clumps of reeds and stop again and again to watch and listen. There were birds and rising fish to see

and there was always the changing water to watch as it eddied round rocks or swept smoothly along in the deep places.

Slowly, as though from a half-remembered dream at night, she came to have a picture of the river as a person. It had long, green hair like feathery weeds and a pale-brown face. Its clothes were a cluster of pieces of cloth, rust-colour and grey-green and white and these swayed and trembled and fluttered as the river moved.

It had a language, too. At night, its rambling, unending talk lulled Jane to sleep. They had moved into the house in late February. Then the river was full and its voice was harsh and loud. 'Listen to the rough wild-water song which rolls the rocks as it rushes along,' it seemed to repeat over and over again until it faded to a low muttering which ran through Jane's dreams.

In April it was quieter. 'From sudden showers in field and lane, the rivers drink spring rain again,' it babbled on and on. In June it was quieter still. 'River run. Never done. All in fun, in the sun,' it murmured. July was hot and dried it up to a narrow stream. 'As still as a snake in the forest's deeps, on sandbanks dry the river sleeps,' it whispered.

'What do you find to do down there all the time?' her mother asked. Jane told them about what she saw and about the changing voice of the river with its rhymes that sent her to sleep.

'It sounds a bit eerie to me,' said her father. 'You're an odd child.'

Martin, however, took it more seriously. One or two nights a week he would go over to his friend Nick's house. He cycled the short way along the lane, across the old bridge and up the steep field beyond. If Jane was by the river and he spotted her on his way to Nick's, he would leave his bike in the lane and walk down to talk to her.

At first he just teased her but soon her interest in the river seemed to worry him. He warned her about getting wet and catching cold and then he said that the river water was dirty. Playing near it could make her ill.

On late October evenings there was usually a mist over the water and under the trees. One evening Martin said, 'You've got an obsession about this place.'

'What's an obsession?' she asked.

'You can't keep away,' he told her. 'The river calls you. It's put a spell on you.'

'I know,' she said. 'I like it.'

'I don't,' he said. 'It's creepy. This time of year it gives me the shivers. Kids drown in rivers like this. You want to keep away from here.'

'No, I don't,' she said.

Later that autumn she started to get up just before it was light and go down to the river. One morning, she found that Martin had followed her.

'You're crazy,' he said angrily. 'Look how deep it runs after all the rain. If you don't stop coming down here, I'll speak to Mum and Dad. They'll stop you. Come back to the house. I don't like you being down here all alone. It could be dangerous.'

She went back with him. She felt he might be right. There had been a lot of rain that autumn. The river was higher up its banks than she had ever seen it. It looked powerful and treacherous as it surged along.

Jane kept away after Martin's warning and for the first time, listening to it at night, she felt uneasy. Now it was hard to fit words to its confused, continuous roar and it kept her awake rather than soothing

74

her. Half-dozing, half-dreaming one night she thought she heard it repeating hoarsely, 'The girl I called and not the brother, but if not one I'll have the other.'

It scared her full awake at the time but she almost forgot about it until that evening.

It had rained very hard all day. She had got wet coming home from school and it took her some time to get dry and change her clothes. Martin had gone to see Nick. Her parents were not yet home and she was quite alone in the house. The rain had stopped and, as she looked at the darkness outside, the thought of the river gave her a creepy feeling. She could hear it clearly but she certainly did not feel like going down there. As she stood at the front-room window she could see the lighted room behind her reflected in the glass. She blinked and yawned. She had gone to sleep late the night before. Suddenly she shivered.

The river's roar was forming words in her head again, 'I give you now the river's warning. Its chill, dark force the bridge is storming. The waves' cold clutch will drag him down and hold him deep enough to drown.' She gasped and stepped back. A head and shoulders loomed dimly outside the window. The face was pale brown and its long green hair moved and stirred. It gazed at her and then it smiled unpleasantly.

It vanished as headlights lit up the garden plot outside. Her parents had arrived. She ran out to them.

'Quick!' she shouted. 'The bridge! There's been an accident.'

They did not ask questions. She bundled into the car and they drove up the lane. When they stopped, the headlights lit up the steep farm track down the field across the river and the sagging, broken bridge. A fallen tree, carried by the force of the water, had knocked out two of the supports.

They could see Martin's bike coming speeding across but they had no time to warn him and he braked too late.

He plunged straight off the bridge into the white, tumbling water. His father was out of the car in the same instant and in the river after him. They were both washed yards downstream before, gasping and coughing, they reached the bank. Jane and her mother helped them to safety.

It was a week before the water went down enough for them to rescue the bike. Afterwards, when they had recovered and rung the police to report the bridge, there were explanations. Nick had been out when Martin had got to his house and Martin had come straight back again. In the rain, which had re-started, and the darkness he had not seen the wrecked bridge until the sudden glare of the head-lights had lit it up. In the next second he was falling.

'I thought I'd had it,' he admitted.

'Brr! So did I,' shivered his mother.

'How did you know about the bridge?' asked Jane's father.

'I just knew,' she said. She simply couldn't tell them why and though they looked at her a bit strangely they did not question her about it.

It was a long time before she could get to sleep that night. The river thundered distantly through the patter of rain on her window. It had no words for her but it sounded angry. In the spell of dry weather that followed, the roaring of the swollen waters grew quieter. It was several nights, though, before she stopped lying awake and afraid.

She did not go near the river again. After Christ-

76

mas her father got promotion and they moved to
the suburb of a town. There was no river near the
house and Jane did not look for one.

Looking at the story again

1 What sound was there in the new house that Jane
could not get used to?
2 What were Jane's parents like?
3 What sort of a girl was Jane?
4 How did she make herself feel better after she had
been in trouble?
5 When was the river's voice most quiet?
6 Who thought it might be dangerous for Jane to go
so often to the river?
7 How did the river look in autumn?
8 Where had Martin gone on that evening when
Jane was alone in the house?
9 Whose face seemed to look in at Jane through the
window that evening?
10 What did she think the river was going to try to
do?
11 What happened to the bridge?
12 Why could Martin not stop when he reached it?
13 How easy was it for Martin's parents to rescue
him?
14 Why might the river have sounded angry to Jane
that night?

Words

1 'fascinated'; 'efficient' – use these two words in two
sentences of your own.
2 'As still as a snake' – complete these sentences with
interesting comparisons of your own:
    The night was as quiet as. . .

The town centre was as crowded as. . .
The dog was as hairy as. . .
The room was as noisy as. . .

3 Which word in the story means 'something you can't stop thinking about' or 'something that you can't leave alone'? It is used by Martin. Find it and write it down. Be careful to spell it correctly.

Writing

1 Have you a favourite place in the town or in the country that you like to visit? Write a description of it and say why you like being there.

2 Write a poem called 'Odd One Out' or 'Loneliness'. It need not rhyme.

3 Write a story about two children who go away for a holiday together. One is dreamy and untidy; the other always plans ahead and likes things neat. Where do they go? What happens on the holiday? Do they get on each other's nerves?

4 Write a story about an accident. It could be something that happened to you or it could be a story you make up.

5 Where would you most like to live? Do you enjoy where you are living now or can you imagine a more enjoyable place? Write about it.

6 'He found himself outside the building again. Something always drew him back there. This time, though, he would go in.' What was the building – a house, an old castle or a museum? What did he find inside – a pleasant surprise or something else? Use the three sentences as the start of your own story.

Ghost Quiz

Score 2 if you know the answer. Score 1 if you have to find it by looking back in the book:

The Ghost Who Liked Babies

1 What was the name of the brainy boy?
2 How many babies of Mrs Rogers were buried at the age of one?
3 What did the reporter think that the 'kid' had come to see him about?

Dream Dog

1 Why did Ray and Hickey tease Tony about his name?
2 What errand was Tony sent on?
3 What was the colour of the dog?

The Ghost Who Sneezed

1 What was Tom's other name?
2 Which two doctors did he go to see?
3 What did the American lady jump out of?

The Old Schoolmaster

1 What did the children drink at Mr Samsworth's house?
2 What did Mr Samsworth's ghost first help Matthew to do?
3 Where was the outing to?

Please Don't Haunt Here

1 What was the name of the ghost in the garage?
2 Where had he come from?
3 Who was his 'mate'?

The House On The Moor

1 Why were the children on the moors?
2 What clothes did the old lady dress in?
3 What type of car came to the rescue of the children?

The Ghostly Computer

1 Why did Miss Wade take the program home at the weekend?
2 What did the first number mean?
3 What did D6 mean?

The Midnight Horses

1 Which child loved the countryside? Sheila or Rachel?
2 How many horses were there?
3 Name one strange thing Rachel noticed about the horses.

Ghost Spray

1 What did Susan think might happen to her mattress?
2 What was the name of the book that Susan read at Uncle Alan's?
3 Was there a smell to the ghost spray?

The River

1 What did the river say in February?
2 How did Martin travel to Nick's?
3 How many river rhymes are there in the story?